# THAT'S LIFE

ANIKA SAHA

ISBN 979-8-89610-654-8

*Dedication*

*Dedicated to the Almighty, by whose Grace, I express my feelings, my younger sister Anushka who is my best friend, my parents and my grandparents.*

# *Preface*

*"THAT'S LIFE" is a collection of poetry and prose about the journey of life of a teenager. This book is a collection of poems, each with different emotions, each poem dealing with the different mood swing, the hope and frustrations of a growing teenager.*

*The book takes readers through the journey of the bitter sweet moments in the life of a teenager. This book is all about the trials and tribulations that teenager has to face while growing up in this world. Through this journey, high and low, ups and downs, there is "Life" for those who believe in it.*

*Life is a challenge in itself more so for a growing teenager experiencing the various emotions the life has to offer. This book while presenting varied emotions of life promises triumph for those who believe in eternal hope.*

*"THAT'S LIFE" explores the various emotions that a growing teenager experiences and prepares the reader to accept life as it is. Life is all about experiencing the various emotions, accepting Life as it is and live a contented life.*

# Index

# About the Author

*Anika is a determined teenager raised in Indian values system wanting to explore the world with eternal hope. She has a great sense of humor and can turn any tense situation into a happy one. In the most impression able years of a life she expresses her emotions by writing poems. The poems reflect the emotions of a benevolent empathic girl going through the difficult period of teenage.*

*Her deep understanding of fellow human beings' frustrations, fears, and despairs of this age has resulted in collection of the poems. The poems reflect the strong emotions of a sensitive mind who is not willing to cower down, who is willing to struggle and hope that all shall be well. When we have nothing to fight for, it is our eternal hope that gives us the strength to go on. This book is all about accepting life as it is.*

*Hoping to help fellow teenagers going through the difficult journey of life with eternal hope what is this book all about.*

*Believe...... That's Life.*

# Famine

*Dying of hunger and strife,*
*Poison has become ripe with life,*
*The crops stand destroyed by the Sun's fiery eyes,*
*Not a drop of water in those empty skies.*

*The wells lie dry, scorched to the Sun's blaze,*
*A mirage of hope, blindly we chase,*
*The trees are parched, dried to stone,*
*The land stands barren, scattered with bones.*

*Famine has ravaged these lands once fair,*
*Death's despair now flies through the air,*
*Men lay dying, their lips readily placed,*
*At the cup of water, death's poison laced.*

*The crimson Sun now leaves the skies,*
*To the accompaniment of the dead men's cries.*
*The wounded skies now cry in pain,*
*Weeping those tears of lifeless rain, all in vain.*

# Silent Footprints

*Footprints follow me upon the sandy shore,*
*A silent man walks behind with the sea's roar,*
*Clear & stark, the impressions stand,*
*Everlasting it seems upon the sand.*

*Who is it who walks behind?*
*Whom, I never seem to find,*
*Whose steps are silent like the dead man's voice.*
*Whose gaze is empty like a prisoner's choice.*

*I turn my head to see,*
*The spirit of the sea.*
*Alas! I see nothing but mist,*
*Nothing but emptiness seems to exist.*

*Now I understand, I walk alone,*
*Haunted by the ghost, long gone past,*
*The sand bears the mark of his solitary stone,*
*Nothing but the memories, truly lasts.*

ᔓ✽ᔓ

# Snow white fields

The snow-white fields covered with snow,
Beneath the sun seemed to glow,
Frosted leaves hang from the trees,
Hanging limp, despite the breeze.

For miles and miles as far eyes can see,
Encounter thee, this frosty sea.
With frozen beauty these frigid winds fly,
Dancing a ballet in the cloudless sky.

The fair lady winter, she tosses her hair,
Letting the pretty flakes fall through the air,
Her soft cold hands have blessed these lands,
Covered in sheets of pure white sand.

Snow white fields, I remember them now,
A broken memory still found somehow,
Through the desert howl, I yearn to hear,
The frozen whispers that fly through the air.

# Caravan's Journey.

Dust of sands dance in the air,
Through which travel the Caravans' fair,
Their iron wheels kissing the soil,
The oxen hooves drenched in sweaty toil.

Covered tents pulled by countless mules,
Desire & determination, their only fuel,
A guild of men, women & children strong,
Travel on, on this journey long.

Oh, the caravan gently traverses the land,
In their wake churning the ever-shifting sand,
Under the sun's glare, fierce bright light,
The caravan's search for a future bright.

The caravan rolls & rolls through the green hills,
Till they finally come to a standstill,
Finally in the land of promises, they rest,
The caravans have now ceased to walk abreast.

ぐ✽ぐ

# Victory

Oh Piper! Pipe that song again,
Lift your fiddle tonight,
Victory we've won, our enemies slain,
Our king has won this fight.

Bring out the shots of merry wine,
The feasts been laid bare,
Dressed in jewels & silk so fine,
A merry daze without a care.

By the fire's flame we wildly dance,
Drowned in shots of a merry trance.
We raise our cups to proudly toast,
Of victories & conquests to forever boast.

"A toast to the country,
A toast to the king,
A toast to the victory,
Proudly we sing."

ᔓ✽ᔓ

# *Fate is a fickle mistress*

*Darling fate,*
*What a fickle mistress you are,*
*You think, you contemplate!*
*The odds of every hour.*

*You shroud my brow in leaves of gold,*
*Whispering poisonous stories untold,*
*Then you leave me alone to drown,*
*A wretched outcast of this town.*

*Fate, you turn & twist my way,*
*To every chime led astray,*
*You hold my hand & then let go,*
*Cutting a tree that started to grow.*

*What a fickle mistress you are, my love*
*Yet you tear my heart, dear dove,*
*The odds demand your presence one more time,*
*Darling fate, you change to every chime.*

# Lying dead in the tulip fields

Lying dead in the tulip fields,
A soft wreath covers her weary head,
A gentle spirit has left to yield,
She sees the light shining ahead.

Rivers of blood water these sands,
A knife left clutched in her dying hands,
The blade inches deep into her heart,
Its searing pain left her broken apart.

The singing crows now come to brood,
At the job unfinished, left so crude,
The tired eyes refuse to see,
The soul has drowned in the forever seas.

A life lived in vain, without a complain,
Dying with nothing but searing pain,
Those who she thought as family,
Left her to rot, cruelly.

ᔓ✽ᔓ

# Forest road

*Golden leaves, they seem to fall,*
*From the firs & oaks towering tall,*
*On the little path on the forest road,*
*Where millions, forever strode.*

*Trees are thick, kissing together,*
*A serene haze from the weary weather,*
*The sun begs to shine through its shade,*
*The polished road turned to a glade.*

*Once laid with perfect cobbled stones,*
*Now lies broken covered with dust and bones,*
*Once the path of men for thousand centuries,*
*Forgotten, ravaged with wild born trees.*

*No one travels no more,*
*It's now a forgotten folklore,*
*Once it led to a bustling city,*
*Now in ruins, left in pity.*

∽✽∽

# Wipe your tears

*Wipe your tears little girl,*
*Close your eyes tonight,*
*Your weary mind in a frightful swirl,*
*Please, let go of this fight.*

*Find solace in the silence of your room,*
*It's silence deafening like an empty tomb,*
*Let its cold hands tuck you in bed,*
*Let the darkness hold your tired head.*

*Let the evening light dance for your pleasure,*
*Let it hold your heart.*
*Remember these memories forever to treasure,*
*Let the shadows play their part.*

*Close your eyes to let this music through,*
*The silence weaves it, just for you.*
*This silence is golden, its moments true,*
*Let the darkness sing its song for you.*

# Forest Spirit

*I once saw in the woods,*
*In this dark, cold forest,*
*A little red riding hood,*
*Who with the trees walked abreast.*

*The trees rustle these sounds,*
*Of stories lost and found,*
*For her, the winds pick up a song,*
*A wild dance raging strong.*

*The fawns skitter close,*
*To her gentle walking form,*
*Holding a single red rose,*
*Like a rock, weathering a storm.*

*The shadows guide her way,*
*Her gentle form rippling away,*
*The darkness hides the grandeur of her face,*
*She vanishes now, without a trace.*

ℭ✿ℭ

# The last flower

She asked her father for a flower sweet,
Just before her heart ceased to beat,
A simple rose would do alone,
A single rose on her little gravestone.

O my little girl, ask for something else,
Spoke her father clutching her little hand,
For you I'd walk through thousand hells,
Yet how'd I will find a rose in this desert land?

"Then father, would you hug me close,
So, I may forget my dear rose",
Said she, her voice turning faint,
Her feverish eyes turning quaint.

I can't see tears frame your face,
Cannot let them diminish your grace,
Her father promised to finish the task,
But a little promise, he begged to ask.

*"Promise me, you'll stay strong, love,*
*Live on till I return, dove."*
*I'll find for what your heart seeks,*
*Live for me please, just one more week.*

*Goodbye father, was all he heard,*
*A gentle soft little word.*
*For the desert howl drowned the rest,*
*And the desert sands danced abreast.*

*And so, he walked mile after mile,*
*Braving the weather cruel and vile.*
*Mirages glittering in deathly sands,*
*Not an oasis across the land.*

*On & on he walked on still,*
*In the harsh sun with a hopeful will,*
*Until he stumbled upon a garden of rose,*
*Towering tall, it strangely rose,*

*Thirsty & tired, he fell on the burning sand,*
*On the parched earth, the rose less land,*
*A mirage of his daughter swam before his sunken eyes,*
*A dead girl's dying father laid beneath the cruel skies.*

*Was it all in vain?*
*All the pain,*
*A daughter's dying wish,*
*Only a father's heart can bleed to fulfill the promise.*

ꕥ

# I cannot

*I cannot drink the poison you pour,*
*I cannot be your slave no more,*
*I cannot stay still while you shake me to the core,*
*I will not stay quiet anymore.*

*I will not hang my head in shame,*
*My heart is wild, no more tame,*
*I do not cower to your words & leers.*
*My heart is empty of fears & tears.*

*I am no longer yours,*
*Your kisses, I cannot endure,*
*I am wild, I am free,*
*I belong to the endless sea.*

*It was not love but a bondage,*
*Pure disrespect & indifference,*
*Today I break free of this cage,*
*For me, to feel the loving difference.*

# Let it be.

Let the waters turn high,
Let the sun dip down low,
Let the caged lapwings fly,
And let the green grass grow.

Let the river flow with steadfast prowess,
Mingling with the wind's soft caress,
Let them fly, Oh! The pretty fireflies,
Oh! Let them soar to the skies.

Let the wind sing a merry song,
For which the earth has yearned so long,
Let the dancers of light dance in the northern skies,
Let the crimson hue paint the glorious sunrise.

Let it be, touch it not,
Let the sea churn and gently froth,
The glorious sky and the glorious sand,
Let the light dance upon the calling land.

ᘛ✽ᘚ

# Gemini

I want to cut off these chains,
That bind my soul tight,
A ghostly image forever pertains,
I want to let go of this fight.

I am tired, going downhill,
Lost the strength in my weakened will,
Weakened by the conflicting voices,
Driven by lifeless, empty choices.

A whirlwind through the back of my mind,
Leaving me tumbling in the darkness blind,
Fear grips me as if a lover's embrace,
Its chains through me, I can't face.

In my mind a battle begins anew at dawn,
Forever this war song plays on and on,
Thrashing seas of worries forever,
I want it to stop for peace so dear.

*Is it too much to ask for a moment of peace,*
*A little lullaby and a life of ease,*
*I simply ask for when I close my eyes,*
*A wish to see truth against a canvas of lies.*

*I wish to hear my voice strong and true,*
*Laced not with pity, nor with rue.*
*I want courage, a chivalrous heart,*
*A story to begin from the start.*

# The Broken Queen

*I must walk this road,*
*I must till these fields,*
*I must pick up my sword,*
*My crown, my shield.*

*I cannot cower under the chairs,*
*I cannot hide my face,*
*I cannot wish for all the stares,*
*To vanish, without a trace.*

*I cannot close my eyes,*
*And wish for my burdens to go away,*
*My heart is held by self-told lies,*
*It cannot risk going astray.*

*Oh, the queen has much on her plate,*
*Her path is tainted by fate,*
*Though free and yet in chains,*
*The queen is whole, yet broken again.*

# Tested limits.

*When the hour is nigh,*
*And the moon shines high,*
*Then memories broken and torn,*
*Crawl out of my eyes, once again reborn.*

*Maybe when you look at me, you cannot tell the difference,*
*Cannot look underneath this pretense,*
*But in my eyes if you search hard enough,*
*You will find a wounded soul, tired of these ways so rough.*

*You know what quaint thing it is,*
*Faking a smile just to appease,*
*It's easier than to explain,*
*The cause of your tears when in denial of persisting pain.*

*Sometimes I do not understand this heart of mine,*
*Tired and broken, yet beating fine,*
*Why does it beat with a frantic worry?*
*What's the reason my eyes refuse to dry?*

*Why do I exist in this tuneless symphony?*
*In a world that's ever so phony,*
*Shall I give up, let it go?*
*Answer to which I still don't know.*

*If I ever broke apart in front of one and all,*
*Know that the dam has crumbled to fall,*
*For my limits would have reached that fateful day,*
*Tired of crying alone forever, "Help me", all my parched lips would say.*

❦

# Distant friends.

*Maybe we are lost in the crossroads of fate,*
*Maybe we are drowned in the seas of expectations great,*
*Maybe we searched for something that isn't there,*
*Looking for signs in the skies all bare.*

*Perhaps we forgot the purpose of life,*
*While we got entangled in the arms of strife,*
*Perhaps all of us turned deaf to the voices in our hearts,*
*Perhaps tis the reason we all fell apart.*

*Once we used to be friends I think,*
*All that vanished in just a blink,*
*Each separated by an expanse so wide,*
*These self-created boundaries we each abide.*

*Maybe once we cared for each other's pain,*
*Perhaps none of us were ever so vain,*
*Alas! These questions hold now no value,*
*For between us are now seas of rue.*

ᔓ❃ᔓ

# A song for the lonely whore.

*She was a little girl when she was sold,*
*To vile masters, for four pieces of gold,*
*For her dark hair and fuller lips,*
*She was thrown to the whorehouse's grips.*

*And there she grew, that lonely whore,*
*Drowning days, hurting away from a sandy shore,*
*She yearned for freedom and her dignity,*
*The little girl who lost her virginity.*

*Then she escaped, that little girl,*
*She gave into time's frightful whirl,*
*She let death drown her deep,*
*So that her eyes may cease to weep.*

*Her tormentors got another,*
*Somebody else's daughter, why bother.*
*A society so timid, so blind,*
*Why would anyone mind?*

# Four shots of wine.

*At the dusty tavern in the darkened night,*
*Four of us sat beneath the moth bitten light,*
*Round the table with the fading shine,*
*Four of us sat with four shots of wine.*

*Ten years hence since that fateful day,*
*When our world turned dark and grey,*
*For a friend turned to a murderous foe,*
*Though for what reason, I still don't know.*

*We four were the thickest of friends, weren't we?*
*Then how come between us, lies leagues of sea,*
*How was the rift born between the closest of hearts?*
*Breaking as forever farther apart.*

*And now we meet after a decade worth distance,*
*To toast on forgiveness or reveal in vengeance,*
*I do not know what this young night will bring,*
*Lying deceit or kind forgiving.*

*The silence was broken by the one who started the fight,*
*Sitting imposing on his chair like a diseased blight,*
*Ego used to reflect in his dark vile eyes,*
*But now in them, I see the raining skies.*

*His trembling lips parted to say,*
*Forgive me brothers for that fate less day,*
*My neck is bare and at your mercy,*
*You may choose to forgive or cut it from its misery.*

*I do not know what magic that mysterious night did play,*
*As if years of harbored vengeance suddenly flew away,*
*A murderous foe turned to the dearest friend,*
*With four shots of wine that night did end.*

# Little girl.

*I promised, I wouldn't break her heart,*
*I promised her happiness from the start,*
*The little girl who lived in me,*
*I promised her, all her eyes could see.*

*I told her, she wouldn't get hurt,*
*I promised her she wouldn't taste dirt,*
*Alas! It was I who pushed her deep,*
*I stood by and let her weep.*

*It was my whips who cut her back,*
*My insults turned her world black,*
*I pushed her into the cold poisoned sea,*
*I broke the little girl who resided in me.*

*I broke her gentle innocent trust,*
*And left her crying on the decaying dust,*
*Through the wretched ways I let her down,*
*In the sea of misery, I left her to drown.*

*That little girl of innocent years,*
*Now lived in a prison of darkened fears,*
*I made her broken and forever bound,*
*That little girl is now no more found.*

✿

# Egoistic desires

I want the beasts to roar my name,
I want to swim in the seas of fame,
I want everything and forever more,
It's my desire to fly and soar.

It may be selfish, this burning desire,
Maybe my ego or my ire,
But I won't stop for I want it all,
I want to be the queen in the glamorous hall.

I cannot satiate this monstrous greed,
I want the power, on glory to feed,
With the crown I wish to extravagantly feast,
Its essence shall feed this feral beast.

Mine are these egoistic desires,
Keeps burning this yearning fire,
I won't stop for I want it all,
I wish to be the Queen in the burning hall.

✻

# Weakness

They said that I was weak,
And perhaps, I thought so too,
But as they stretched on each day of the week,
A question, I had in my mind too.

Was I destined to serve forever?
Could I never wear the crown?
Was I a rock to be trampled and weathered upon?
Would I be forever be looked down upon?

At night I lay watching the hours tick by,
Watching the shadows fleeting fly,
And then I knew what kept me from mine,
Just simply a glass of poisoned wine.

My body may be weak but my mind is not,
I don't care for consequences, distraught and fraught,
A drop of poison will kill my foe,
My enemy alas, will drown in woe.

*My foe is gone and now I have the crown,*
*Now I am the one who from the throne looks down,*
*I may be weak but I have the power,*
*Now, to my gaze all must cower.*

ေ✽ေ

# Lost lover.

Lost to sea,
Your soul stood to be,
Last across the abyss,
Your presence, I miss.

I remember well,
The night where my mind does dwell,
The day we parted,
And you travelled across the waters uncharted.

Since that day,
No other ship returned to the bay,
Not a single sailor came to say,
"Goodbye darling, I'll be away".

Oh! How I waited forever and ever more,
And nursed my heart so sore,
Awaiting your return,
Your presence, I yearn.

*Wasting away,*
*By that lonely bay,*
*I beg death to ease my pain,*
*So I may see you once again.*

ᔓ✾ᔓ

# Secret.

*In the heart garrisoned,*
*Lies a secret imprisoned,*
*From the view so hidden,*
*It's existence completely forbidden.*

*It seeks to escape,*
*From the crevice agape,*
*A secret wishes to speak,*
*Blurted out from the heart so weak.*

*It makes the heart heavy,*
*A burden hard to carry,*
*Yearning to break free*
*In the world to be.*

*The secret in the heart confined,*
*Is a bird left broken and blind,*
*One that longs to be free,*
*To be spoken or not to be.*

# Witch Elm.

*There stands a lone witch Elm,*
*At the darkness's helm,*
*Warnings thus said,*
*Of the trials ahead.*

*It warns of the darkness that lies,*
*On a road where the sun does not rise,*
*It wants all those who dare,*
*Not to venture in the darkness fair,*

*A weary task day in and day on,*
*Warning fools, on and on,*
*Fools who never listen,*
*And seek to walk the road where blood does glisten.*

*Many ventures in,*
*Where the darkness seeps in,*
*Yet non return back,*
*For sense, their hearts, do lack.*

✻

# Undone

*The task is done,*
*It can't be undone.*
*Then why think and worry,*
*And let our souls bury.*

*The war is fought,*
*Glorious or fraught,*
*Worrying will only bring,*
*Sufferings upon its wings.*

*The task is done,*
*It can't be undone, can't be redone,*
*Irreversible stands the notion,*
*Constant unchanging like the rising Sun.*

*The love is gone forever,*
*Maybe it was never there,*
*The indifference, the disrespect, the mistrust,*
*I am done and I must.*

# Down by the bay.

A Glorious day,
By the salty bay,
The waves dance and play,
A symbol of joy in a world that's grey.

The salty breeze blows,
By the palm trees that grows,
The waves break and roar,
The birds fly and soar.

A symbol of serenity,
A picture of tranquility,
A paradise lies by the horizon,
Away from the dark city prison.

I stare longingly ahead,
What a life I have made!
Gone forever are the days,
Too late to mend my ways.

# Melodies.

Give me a violin that I might play,
On and on through the shady day,
And sing songs all through,
Across the days of woe and rue.

Tunes I will string,
And play songs so young in the spring,
In the tunes I will lose my way,
Fall gently into its sway.

Resonance surround,
Gentle tunes all around,
Sweet melodies bind,
The joy in my heart to find.

My tunes are all I got,
In a life so distraught,
Before the strings break,
A symphony is there to make.

ೞ✽ೞ

# Weeping willow

*A Little girl once did sow,*
*Tall and firm, a little willow,*
*With love she did tend,*
*To her love, the willow did bend.*

*It was a pretty sight,*
*The girl's willow in the first light,*
*The girl dancing underneath,*
*Love was in the air to breathe.*

*On a cruel fateful day,*
*The plague took the girl away,*
*The willow waited over the years,*
*In the rain he shed his tears.*

*The tall proud willow,*
*Bent to the grief so mellow,*
*In her absence he wept,*
*Laying a wreath of leaves on her lonely crypt.*

# The journey.

*We traverse this journey,*
*A brilliant cacophony,*
*A sweetened symphony,*
*With love and loss, in harmony.*

*This is the journey of life,*
*With joy and strife,*
*A journey with hurdles profound,*
*Yet light to enjoy abound.*

*Life is graced,*
*With pain and joy, it's laced.*
*That's the beauty,*
*Of this eternal journey.*

*Some of us will fall wayside,*
*Some of us will ride over the tide,*
*"I did my best", all that I would say,*
*In the end on my last day.*

ɞ✽ɞ

# Scarlet.

Scarlet blood seeps,
By the battlefield were all do weep,
The wounded lie,
Underneath the vultures, left to die.

To every blade's slash,
A man did fall,
Open bleeding gash,
In the hearts of all.

On the cold ground bleeding,
For death, praying,
Lies a soldier on the ground,
With scarlet misery all around.

"Our loyalty lies to our king,
His praises we sing,
For him our swords are ready,
For him, we embrace the deathly melody.

*We do not regret or repent,*
*Our blood is well spent,*
*Ready to die times as many,*
*For our King, our home, our country."*

❦

# Painful smile.

I smile through this haze,
With a sorrowful grace,
From your eyes forbidden,
Are my wounds hidden.

I smile at you,
Yet cry, hidden from view,
A facade you see,
A detached shadow of me.

To smile, it burns,
For the darkness I yearn,
The sorrow is my home,
In its embrace, I roam.

Why do I do so?
'Cause I am afraid to let you go.
Won't you ever look beyond my smile?
Won't you ever go the extra mile?

~~*~~

# Cherry blossom.

A lone cherry blossoms sways,
Basking underneath the sun's rays,
Atop the frozen mountain,
It graces the landscape in vain.

The lone blossom is the only one,
To stand where there is none,
Standstill, it stands tall,
Gracing the eyes of one and all.

It sends its roots deep,
Gently down the mountain they creep,
To withstand the cold breeze that blows,
To stand tall when it snows.

No matter the scars which show,
On its tall and splendid boughs,
Alone he does stand,
Like a king upon the frozen land.

ↀ✽ↀ

# Chaos.

*Where the darkness swells,*
*Where the monsters' dwell,*
*Where the Chaos lies untamed,*
*There I stand, a monster unnamed.*

*Where all the gold is dust,*
*Swaddled in the chains of broken trust,*
*Where a wicked tune plays the lute,*
*Mercy! Pleadings upon the flute.*

*Where all light plunges into the darkness,*
*Horror and misery glow in all their starkness,*
*Where malice and envy snake the floors,*
*And vengeance and revenge knock the doors.*

*That's the Chaos of my mind,*
*The Chaos of my heart,*
*Help me for what I hope to find,*
*A small piece of peace to break this storm apart.*

# Why should I apologize.

*Why should I apologize?*
*For the monster I became,*
*Why should I cry a heart?*
*Which bled in the shackles of tame.*

*Why should I collect my heart's shard?*
*Which lies on cold ground, hard,*
*Why should I be with pain and strife?*
*For what became of my life.*

*When no one apologized a single time,*
*For what they turned me into,*
*A monster fit for the tales and rhymes,*
*Those fiends did not say a drop of rue.*

*Betrayed time and again,*
*Forced to live a life of eternal pain,*
*I did no harm, no wrong,*
*Why should I now not sing my own song?*

ↀ✻ↀ

# Snowflake

Here falls the gentle snow flake,
And leave broken stories in its wake,
Journeys so far,
Live in the heart, a painful scar.

Whilst drifting,
When the entire world was sleeping,
I saw misery of the wretched,
In the scenery ahead so stretched.

I saw a wreath,
I saw death,
Of a man so old,
Alone in the wintery cold.

Soon I moved on,
To cities on and on,
Yet wherever I did go,
Their misery, I couldn't forego.

*Was it my doing?*
*My wintery being,*
*That broad pain,*
*To those in the cold so lain.*

*I wish I had stayed,*
*In the clouds overhead,*
*The guilt is heavy,*
*The weight of it, I cannot carry.*

*Punish me God for my crimes,*
*I have hurt them many a times,*
*Unknowing I brought them sorrow,*
*Barred them from their bright tomorrow,*

*Bring in the summer sun,*
*Let over winter, its victory won,*
*Melt the cold away,*
*With the darling sun's golden rays.*

*Let there be warmth and light,*
*The justice is right,*
*In death I will repent,*
*My crimes committed in the years so spent.*

# Witch burning

*Tied to stake,*
*By the bloody lake,*
*Doused in gasoline,*
*In that frightful scene.*

*For false crimes accused,*
*In the Devil's name used,*
*Accused of treason,*
*Without rhyme or reason.*

*Alive caught,*
*Condemned to a fate so fraught,*
*Burned alive,*
*The pain like thousand knives.*

*Flames roar and flourish,*
*My essence they tarnish,*
*I face annihilation,*
*In the God's name, for no reason.*

ꕥ

# Jealousy.

A burning desire,
Like a roaring fire,
That burns within,
And commits me to sin.

A poisonous fiend,
My darling friend,
An essence I breathe,
In my blood jealousy does seethe.

Come my friend tell me sweet words,
Words entirely absurd,
The ones that will turn my mind,
And leave sanity out of reach to find.

I know well, you'll suck me dry,
And leave me in the end to cry,
Still, I cannot forgo your presence,
You are my breath, my very essence.

ഗ✻ഗ

# *Gold mines.*

*Deep under the earth hidden,*
*Lies a treasure forbidden,*
*Gold glitters underneath,*
*Softly across the earth beneath.*

*Sweetly, the mine does call,*
*Welcome's all into his shadow halls,*
*All desperate enough to venture in,*
*Into the rocky halls unseen.*

*The greed of gold,*
*A longing across young and old,*
*Draws the men inside,*
*To wear the darkness does reside.*

*Yet once inside,*
*The darkness wraps with full tide,*
*It crumbles its halls so old,*
*Kills all with a heart of gold.*

∽✽∽

# Runaway

*A hitchhiker stands beneath,*
*The barren trees underneath,*
*A shelter from the pouring rain,*
*That gently washes away all the pain.*

*Upon the barren highway,*
*Stands a lonely runway.*
*An outcast stands alone,*
*Underneath the street light, cold to the bone.*

*Leaving behind,*
*A new home to find,*
*In the eyes, dwell the tears,*
*In the heart, dwells the fear.*

*A daughter of the Earth and the sky,*
*Which tears, brimming the eyes,*
*Undaunting stands a spirit steadfast,*
*In the rain, stands a lonely outcast.*

# Paradise

*Across the vast stretches of land,*
*Glitters the golden sand,*
*The mighty river snakes by,*
*Reflecting the azure sky.*

*Clouds dot the sky overhead,*
*And the sun gleams ahead,*
*The picture of most perfection,*
*Drawn to God's artistic satisfaction.*

*Each leaf gleams,*
*Underneath the golden sun beams,*
*Flowers with the colors bright,*
*Gleam in the first light.*

*A picture so serene,*
*Shrouded in grass so green,*
*Among the waterfalls between,*
*Lies a paradise unseen.*

# Forelone years.

*Dotting the forelone years,*
*A tune of castaway tears,*
*The misery alights,*
*Each and every night.*

*A broken soul does reside,*
*Forelone in the house inside,*
*With no purpose does he roam,*
*In a prison he calls home.*

*He gave up in the years agone,*
*A choice out of pain borne,*
*Sufferings so sweet,*
*Made him give up, made him quit.*

*Now he does dwell,*
*Alone in his lonely hell,*
*Watching the clock tick slow,*
*Living his years, sunken in woe.*

ᔓᔕ✽ᔓᔕ

# Failure.

*Why does my heart beat?*
*With a pain bitter sweet,*
*Why the sorrow my heart can't bury,*
*Why its weight it can't carry?*

*Why do I look to light?*
*Aspire every time to fight,*
*Yet fall and crumble,*
*Every time take a tumble.*

*Crying softly,*
*Despairing bitterly,*
*Lost and in pain,*
*Listening to failure's refrain.*

*I hear it each and every day,*
*Amongst the tears cast away,*
*A song drifts through my mind,*
*Leaving Joy, out of reach to find.*

ᔓᔕ❀ᔓᔕ

# Lashes

*Fifteen, sixteen, seventeen,*
*How many lashes has it been?*
*Eighteen, nineteen, twenty,*
*This bloody back bleeds a plenty.*

*Twenty one, twenty two, twenty three,*
*He drowns in pain's endless sea.*
*Twenty four, twenty five, twenty six,*
*This a sound the healer cannot fix.*

*Twenty seven, twenty eight, twenty nine,*
*Blood spills like drops of wine.*
*Thirty, thirty one, thirty two,*
*His dead body lies amidst the scarlet hue.*

*A handful of rice, a small meal,*
*Betrayed by hunger, the little boy did steal,*
*Was it such a vice?*
*With death he had to pay the price?*

ഗ✽ഗ

# Lowborns

*Cold & weary, the downtrodden way,*
*Through the narrow alleys, the lowborns play,*
*Stench of blood & muck wafts the air,*
*Pulsating & ominous the stench of fear.*

*Death & misery defile this country,*
*The reigns of which belong to poverty,*
*It's the world of lowborns, shunned from light,*
*Untouched by the world, resides their plight.*

*A shade at best of twigs & hay,*
*Neath which, men clamor to lay,*
*For scrapes of bread, blood is spilled,*
*Cries of agony weave on, till the air is stilled.*

*Such is the way, a lowborn grows,*
*A life of misery, a life of woes,*
*From dawn to dusk, a life of torment,*
*Born of clay, dying every moment.*

ᔕ✾ᔕ

# Traveler

Oh traveler! Welcome to the lands gentle and fair.
Worry not about the demon's snare,
Lying, twisted city alleys snake away,
Hold your lantern dear, least you go astray.

Hold your fine jewels to your heart,
Thieves have ruled this land from the start,
Spare not anxious glances to cast behind,
They hide in plain sight, yet are hard to find.

To the low-borns tavern, you are welcome,
Mead & twine and a shanty tune to hum,
Ask for a shade at the best,
Yet hold your dragger close as you rest.

Thieves do not shy to quietly slay,
Sleeping victims burned to clay,
Hide your wares well, whilst you sleep,
Least with the sun your eyes seek to weep.

*Leave at daybreak the Traven's door,*
*For now, you shall reach the city's shore,*
*Bustling carriages jostle their way,*
*Let not the crowd lead you astray.*

*In this life's journey undertaken,*
*Keep your earnings hidden,*
*The riches, the power, the hold,*
*Tis the way of life I'm told.*

ఌ✽ఌ

# Ramshackled

In a ramshackled hut, a poor man did dwell,
His fate he knew well,
Meagre money he had none,
He was an unsightly lonely one.

Yet each day I walked by,
He smiled and said "Hi."
He didn't care of the difference between,
Just another soul inside was seen.

He was willing to help, anyone who would ask,
Never shy, from the most arduous task,
Yet he would ask for no repay,
"Your smile is all I need", he would say.

I wonder when I saw him,
Why he gave into no petty whims,
And always walked with a merry stance,
As if in a sweetened trance.

*Finally, I asked him one fair day,*
*Not anticipating what he would say,*
*I asked him, " Why though in poverty,*
*You possess no sorrow no misery".*

*He replied as gently as he could muster,*
*Wealth he never wished to foster,*
*Who needs a crown on his head?*
*When the stars glisten overhead.*

*I asked him still,*
*If it were by his own free will,*
*Why he took no repay in courtesy,*
*Was it simply gallantry on his novelty?*

*This time he answered,*
*Loudly over all to be heard,*
*Tis no man, who claims reward from the poor,*
*Tis no life, when you look for grandeur.*

ఌ✽ఌ

# Wild Creatures

Do you know, if love were called poison,
We'd drink it still.
If to love were called treason,
We wouldn't stop until we've had our fill.

Even though each heart hides scars,
That refuse to bleed.
Yet we still travel on far,
Searching a rose in a sea of weeds.

No matter how we are steadfast,
This pretense truly never lasts.
We each return as moths flock to light,
To love and lust, Oh! A glorious fight.

Truly our hearts are wild creatures,
With misery etched upon their every feature.
Hence our ribs, our cages to hold their flight,
Lest we shall flock to love, like moths to light.

ઌ✽ઌ

# The Heart

They say to follow your heart,
But when your heart is empty,
When it is broken apart,
Which piece would you dare to follow?

Do you know that tears are words the heart can't say?
The ones, it itself denies.
But when the dam breaks, flooding the bay,
They gently crawl out my eyes.

The queen of hearts, she is a lucky card.
For her heart is whole not pieces of broken shards.
As for us, Oh! Where to begin.
Was ours ever whole? Oh! do tell me when?

Why should we have a heart anyway?
Only to cry out and give away?
'Cause broken hearts still do believe,
There's hope in every life.

ఌ✽ఌ

# Why.

Why?
Why do you lie?
To break my heart,
Into smithereens apart.

Poison you lace,
A fiendish embrace,
A weary haze,
Surrounds my face.

Tell me again,
Why do you leave me in pain?
What's the reason?
Of your high treason.

Why do you betray?
Why do you waylay?
When I give misery to you none,
When I was your faithful and only one.

# Tears of blood.

*Tears from the heart within,*
*Glinting with misery unseen,*
*Blood trickles down the face,*
*With a gentle melancholy grace.*

*With ache so profound,*
*The heart breaks without a sound,*
*From the open gash blood does seep,*
*Leaps to the eye as one does weep.*

*Bound in chains,*
*Of this abysmal pain,*
*Driven insane,*
*Time and time again.*

*The empty bloodshot eyes,*
*Look up to the bleeding skies,*
*Lying upon the blood dripped ground,*
*To death, give in, without a sound.*

✿

# *Dead tears.*

*Dead tears trickle without a sound,*
*Glinting with misery profound,*
*A dead statue does weep,*
*From his sculpted face tears do seep.*

*Everywhere glints the misery profound,*
*Of wretched men all around,*
*Who weep away without a sound,*
*With an aching misery so profound.*

*The statue grieves at what he sees,*
*At poor men hurdled in the shade of trees,*
*Its leaden heart does come alive,*
*When its eyes encounter the inglorious strife.*

*Ironic, is it not?*
*That a statue made of lead and stone,*
*With heart cold to the bone,*
*Breaks in to the misery of the fraught.*

*When we humans cannot ourselves spare,*
*A gentle word or a loving care,*
*The statue with the heart of lead,*
*Was the only one, whose heart, with pity did bleed?*

ധ✽ധ

# Black skies.

The world lies in eternal sleep,
In the darkness so dark and deep,
Where the skies gently weep,
Heralding the gloom that creeps.

The black skies cast over,
Heralding teary shower,
A blank wave washes over,
To where the forelone souls do hover.

The deep black sky spirals into the unknown,
Gently into an abyss, frothing on,
Reflects in her dark eyes the misery profound,
A hazy mist that's around.

The gloom holds a weary embrace,
Over the world that lies in an eternal haze,
The hearts of the wretched all around,
The good lost, evil abound.

ೞ✽ೞ

# Hold my hand.

Hold my hand,
Guide me through,
Through this alley of rue,
Shadowed with sorrow's crimson hue.

Hold me, Lead me,
Through this road worn and old,
Through the thorns and bitter cold,
Littered all over with blood-stained mound.

This journey I call life,
With despair and strife,
For solace I look to thee,
Hold my hand, lead me.

Darling dear, I trust you whole,
Trust you well to light up my soul,
Hope my friend, you light up my way,
In your embrace, the darkness falls away.

∽✽∽

# Azure sky.

Soft clouds flow freely away,
With the gentle breeze that sways,
With weary worry none,
A life glistening with joyous fun.

The azure sky holds in an embrace,
The cloud screened lace,
From where the gentle tears of love do fall,
To the joy of us, one and all.

Yet after the spell of rain,
Glints back up again,
The azure motherly eyes,
Of the pretty azure sky.

Looking up to the azure eyes,
The life below starts to bloom,
The tears of the azure sky,
Brings life back from doom.

ഗ✾ഗ

# The phoenix.

The phoenix sings a weary tune,
Over a grave gleaned with runes,
It sheds a single tear that bleeds,
With scarlet misery, as the phoenix does weep.

Till eternity, he sits still,
By the grave upon the lonely hill,
With profound misery he grieves and cares,
For the lonely grave, rested all bare.

By his master he braves the day,
Through the night in a world that's grey,
A gentle rose he brings every day,
A wreath upon the stone that's grey.

Through the sands of time,
With the misery sublime,
Steadfast he stands upon the crest,
With his master to walk abreast.

*Soon a deadly frost made his way,*
*Where the phoenix rested his head,*
*His head upon the stone, on the grave lay,*
*"I come to you, master", was all that he said.*

❦

# *Failure's refrain*

*The failure's refrain,*
*A cursed bane,*
*Plays alone with the agonizing pain,*
*In the minds of those driven insane.*

*A broken lonely cast away,*
*Heartbroken, by the river does lay,*
*Watching the waves gently eat away,*
*The shores of the forelone bay.*

*Eyes closed he thinks again,*
*Why he suffers the eternal pain,*
*At each time his eyes peace does attain,*
*Plays again the failure's refrain.*

*The aching tunes gently bind,*
*Leaving the heart cold and blind,*
*Gently all life it sucks away,*
*While one weeps by the lonely bay.*

*The fiendish poison leaves behind,*
*A soulless body without a mind,*
*Empty eyes which stare in pain,*
*Listening again and again, to the failure's refrain.*

❧✾❧

# Withered.

*Harsh daylight,*
*And cold frost bite,*
*Snaking vines,*
*Of misery vampirine.*

*Leaves the soul broken,*
*With misery unspoken,*
*The rose lies withered upon the ground,*
*It's little heart breaking without a sound.*

*Tears run dry,*
*With pain a plenty,*
*In a world laced with lies,*
*To embrace the deadly melody.*

*A face shriveled and marred,*
*A heart broken and scared,*
*A victim of eternal pain,*
*Lies a soul withered and slain.*

# Windflower.

*When this body is done,*
*When the reel of time has spun,*
*Burn me in the molten fire,*
*This, only this, is my heart's desire.*

*My spirit shall be free,*
*Flying over the seven seas,*
*Bound by no chains, no shackles,*
*I shall die free, untouched by manacles.*

*Like a dandelion I shall flow,*
*Carried by the breeze with its gentle blow,*
*Free from the worldly ties,*
*Alone I shall fly.*

*Will I look back, repent?*
*For the deeds undone, time unspent,*
*In time my own deeds I shall face,*
*For me death is the final solace.*

ᔓᔕ✻ᔓᔕ

# Snow storm.

*The snow storm winds its way down,*
*Upon the fragile little town,*
*Its arms raised open and wide,*
*To swallow the little town with full tide.*

*The strong winds herald in welcome,*
*The snow king's carriage in a study hum.*
*In his fury the winds do rage,*
*Dancing to the melody of eternal carnage.*

*The helpless houses shiver in fright,*
*While the bare trees weep in plight,*
*For the storm makes each and all,*
*Beg for mercy, at his feet, do fall.*

*As the icy thorns bite our skin,*
*We recount our many sins,*
*Shivering by the fire place,*
*In its warmth filled embrace.*

*Soon comes the tardy spring,*
*With hope upon its wing,*
*Driving away the winter's despair,*
*Comes the gentle lady fair.*

ళ✽ళ

# Solace.

*In an eternal haze,*
*Death is your only solace,*
*In its gentle embrace,*
*You will find your rightful place.*

*As outcast in the world you stay,*
*Lonely by the eternal bay,*
*Bleeding eyes stare away,*
*Lost through the course of day.*

*Aching eyes cry in pain,*
*Reveled in the cursed bane,*
*Waiting for the ache to wane,*
*The gash rips open again and again.*

*Closing forever his eyes, in a gentle sleep,*
*Bleeding whilst he weeps,*
*He falls into the gentle embrace,*
*In those arms of death, he finds solace.*

# Thorns

*Its weary arms do embrace,*
*A rose in a screen of lace,*
*Its thorny arms fast and steady,*
*Hold the throne of the daintily lady.*

*It braves the weather strong,*
*Humming about its work to a weary song,*
*To protect the rose that does reside,*
*Among the shield wall of thorns inside.*

*It cries not at the curses spoken,*
*Stands loyal with the promises, unbroken,*
*It cries never with pain or strife,*
*For his lady, give up his life.*

*Do the thorns live in vain?*
*Inflicting pain, nothing to gain,*
*The beauty of the rose blooms bright,*
*'Cause of a cursed soul, doing what's right.*

ᔓ✽ᔓ

# *Regret.*

*Regret,*
*A dark jewel beset,*
*Set deep within the heart,*
*Gently breaking it slowly apart.*

*Gentle pain in the mind does start,*
*Gently ripping the life apart,*
*Great misery in the heart is seen,*
*Reflecting the pain in the heart unseen.*

*Oh why, oh why?*
*Did I ever lie?*
*Oh, why in lust of greed,*
*Did I plant the hateful seed?*

*The bank of guilt wreaks my mind,*
*Leave me ever so hurt and blind,*
*Oh, please spare, amnesty,*
*Someone, please forgive me.*

*Oh, the road of remorse,*
*Is too wretched to traverse,*
*Oh regret!*
*Is it the dark jewel beset?*

ᔕ✽ᔕ

# Woe.

Life is Oh so....,
Sunken deep in woe,
Alone and lonely,
With the darkness so homely.

What a sad little affair,
Leaving the life utterly bare,
Afraid of the painful whips that fall,
On the backs of wretched, one and all.

From the world unseen,
Great misery dwells within,
Shunned without a sound,
Dwells the grief profound.

Deep inside,
The Grief does reside,
A seed nursed to grow,
A tree darkened with woe.

*Soon grief does turn,*
*With hatred it burns,*
*No more does it weep with misery,*
*Turns to a heart with no sympathy.*

ଓଓ✾ଓଓ

# Moonlit daze.

*The moon throws of its wintery shades,*
*Over the empty silent glade,*
*The clouds of silence weave their way,*
*Over the glorious starry bay.*

*The moon casts of her darkened veil,*
*From where peeks the lady fair,*
*Her gentle face soft and pale,*
*Holds to grandeur the silent air.*

*In the moonlit field springs forth the sounds,*
*Of singing crickets all around.*
*Who sing through praises of boundless glory,*
*Of the crescent damsel in this story.*

*Whilst the lamplights flicker above the streets,*
*While a lone ranger sits beneath,*
*No robin now flies by no more,*
*For the mockingbird now takes to soar.*

*Since ages who didn't endure,*
*The moon's silvering allure,*
*The murderous passion comes in a haze,*
*In the veiled moonlit daze.*

❧✽❧

# Songbird.

Once a little song bird did rise,
With wings, a gleam to the endless skies,
The deary world she wished to fill,
Which song, so she kept on singing still.

Her tunes did gently bind,
Enchanted each and every mind,
With love she did sing,
The tunes danced upon her wings.

Fleeting an arrow pierced her heart,
Breaking all her dreams apart,
Yet she kept on and on,
With the deathly melody of her song.

To sing on, her voice did tremble,
As her heart, dreams all crumbled,
Do listen just one last time,
To this gentle broken loveless rhyme.

ᔓ✽ᔓ

# The Masterpiece.

*Not a neat brushes' stroke,*
*Not a haunting beauty bespoke,*
*Nor a fair lady prime,*
*Or boundless glory sublime.*

*Know the canvas bears none of those,*
*But holds a simple red rose,*
*One that blooms from the heart of stone,*
*Its fiendish thorns upon the barren bones.*

*Painted by no painter so great,*
*With no profound glory to fate,*
*From the depth of heart masterpiece was born,*
*A glory amidst the pretty scorns.*

*Love lost but not forgotten,*
*Alive, though beaten,*
*Few simple strokes from memory,*
*My eternal love, I refuse to bury.*

# Sand and stone

*Write the heart's story,*
*Upon the coldhearted stone,*
*Write all that's there, without worry,*
*Upon the everlasting sandy shore.*

*Write all that you fear,*
*Your anguish, your tears,*
*Those the wind shall blow away,*
*Away from sight, Oh, so far away.*

*Write your joy, fill your heart,*
*Upon whom none can break apart,*
*From eons so long, with the tide,*
*They stand alone alongside the time.*

*For whence age comes your way,*
*And you fall into times sway,*
*Your heart shall beat with all you hold dear,*
*Not your tears nor your darkened fears.*

*For your pillars of sand,*
*They did not stand,*
*With the wind the sands blew away,*
*Leaving the solitary rocks upon the bay.*

ഗ✻ഗ

# A little Plastic heart.

Come back to me,
Please play with me,
Why did you break apart?
My little plastic heart.

I am a toy of plastic and paint,
My heart still beats with the sound, soft and faint,
It too does feel the pain,
Of the wounds inflicted again and again.

You left me to rot,
In the darkness cold and fraught,
Turned away from your sight,
Shunned away from daylight.

How could you forget a friend so dear?
When you hugged me in your anguish and fears,
Who holds no importance to you no more?
Who still sits by, nursing her heart so sore.

*You forgot me, I could never,*
*You broke me, I won't ever,*
*You broke it, broke it apart,*
*My quaint little plastic heart.*

ഗ✾ഗ

# Assassin.

A piercing call you will hear tonight,
Of a lapwing singing out of sight,
With the cloak of darkness she does walk,
Among the devils with chaos amok.

In her wake, cries of mercy you'll listen,
In her wake, blood does glisten,
She is the red rose who sits on the throne,
Of slivered thorns and bones.

Her dagger cuts the night,
Whilst her face is out of sight,
Her breath whispers with snakes,
Her footsteps echo by the stakes.

The moonlight lights up her way,
All fall gently into Her's sway,
Sharp and swift in an alleyway dark,
She'll come behind her unfaithful mark.

*She'll touch not an innocent soul,*
*Though her heart is as black as coal,*
*Her eyes seek out her prey abound,*
*A man of sins is killed without a sound.*

*Her heart holds no compassion,*
*For she kills with furious passion,*
*Sitting gently upon the towers high,*
*She smiles when the lapwings cry.*

# Show me.

*Show me the grace in an unfinished tune,*
*Show me a gentle shade in the mid of noon,*
*Show me hope in the sea of despair,*
*Show me the courage in the depths of fear.*

*Standing alone in a crowd of war,*
*Show me light, shining afar,*
*Of peace who gently breathes,*
*Standalone amongst those unruly weeds.*

*Find my place where I belong,*
*To finish this unfinished song,*
*Send the rain in this desert of sand,*
*I am lost, Gods!, please hold my hand.*

*My ignorant eyes stay blind,*
*Love and light they do not find,*
*Lead me through this haze of darkness,*
*Find me the tune of happiness.*

*I cannot see even in plain sight,*
*Oh God! Show me hope, the shining light,*
*Find my shore in this stormy sea,*
*Grant me a serenity of the shady tree.*

ಌ❃ಌ

# Broken chains.

The scars rub red and raw,
My cold heart, they did thaw,
The fire was lit once again,
Braving the pain, the falling rain.

The eyes opened wide and bright,
Craving the dawning light,
From the caravan of lonely despair,
The desolate filthy snare.

Emerged a gentle spark,
In a world that's cold and dark,
A phoenix rose from its lifeless ashes,
In splendid grandeur with bleeding gashes.

Soaring up to the burning sun,
Each beat of wings was a victory won,
From the darkened depths flew into the air,
The kingdom's own rightful heir.

ಌ✽ಌ

# The Gambler

*She plays a feral gambler's game,*
*Betting gold to her name,*
*Neatly her fingers guide the dice,*
*A slave to her endless vice.*

*Over the thin line she does walk,*
*By the Caravan with riches amok,*
*She fears not a tumble nor fall,*
*As she bewitches one and all.*

*The Gambler plays her golden stance,*
*Cheating defeat at every chance,*
*Luck creeps over her gloved hands,*
*Her golden smile seeps through her golden strands.*

*With a haughty stance she collects her gold,*
*The mistress of her trade so old,*
*The Gambler tosses once again,*
*A delight to the endless pain.*

❦

# *Slithering poison*

*A little prick, as blood spurs down,*
*What's this? I gently frown.*
*Whose fangs did kiss my hand?*
*Crimson red in gentle strands.*

*I wonder whilst I suck the bite,*
*When suddenly my throat feels tight,*
*My head swims in a gentle daze,*
*My eyes stare back at this glorious haze.*

*Oh, I fall to the ground,*
*My eyes burning with ache profound,*
*The snake's venom has reached my heart,*
*Its slithering chains breaking it apart.*

*I gasp for the last snitches of air,*
*My head swims in the depths of fear,*
*My eyes stare back lifeless and whole,*
*For the slithering poison has taken my soul.*

# Dance of woe.

Love, learn to dance to my whims,
Learn to obey,
Protest not to what I say,
Tarry not of what I ask.

Learn to dance to my will,
Hope not, if you do still,
I command you,
Through and through.

My life will touch your skin,
Least you commit your sin,
Simply give me a chance,
Let me take your hand to dance.

Woefully I shall bind you tight,
Binding your wings yearning for flight,
Betray me naught,
Least repercussions be fraught.

*Swear to me your utmost loyalty,*
*Fear not of my cruelty,*
*I shan't hurt you, give me a chance,*
*Let me take your hand to dance.*

❧✾❧

# Handmaiden

Quiet, discrete, she slaves all day,
In the king's castle by the bay,
Taunted and jeered day in and day out,
With grim and mud all about.

With the filthy mop the handmaiden does walk,
To the princess's chamber with jeers amok,
Her proud red lips kiss the hand,
Of the fair lady of this land.

She places the crown upon the queen's head,
Heart filled with anger, tears did bleed,
How could she, her mother's daughter,
Place the crown upon her father's butcher.

The queen's eye bled not with sympathy,
Her cruel smile flickers not with pity,
The frozen heart gleamed with glee,
Upon the ever-bloodier sea.

*Once she was a princess of great beauty,*
*Held by her folk with utmost duty,*
*She was not a handmaiden but the pride of the land,*
*Many did seek her graceful hand.*

*Now what is she but just a slave,*
*Bound to the witch against her will,*
*Her life a mess of sorrowful daze,*
*She lives on hoping until.*

*No Prince was destined to her fate,*
*Though she did try to wait,*
*Only death was there to ease her pain,*
*She gave in to its gentle refrain.*

# She became something wild.

Wild and feral, her heart lies free,
Born of thorns and brambles,
In the hearts of trees.

Caged naught in the bars of gold,
She breaks through free,
With her heart so cold.

With the daggers that drove again and again,
She walks on fire,
Through the endless pain.

She let's not fall the weakened tears,
Least tyrants should see,
Her anguish and fears.

She utters not a single cry,
Whilst the whips fall,
On her back awry.

*Abandoned as a child,*
*She walked on the fateless road,*
*Where rivers of crimson flowed,*

*Through the darkness she stood up tall,*
*Proud, she stood alone in the hall,*
*Her feral heart, a child no more, she became something wild.*

❧❦❧

# Home sweet home.

Italy, Rome, Athens, Greece.
All seem to me same apiece,
None's towers and city meadows,
Compares to those barny shadows,

At home we have just a little field,
Where the rows of wheat gently yield,
Gentle food to eat our fill,
Reaping, reaping forever until.

At home we have those rolling hills,
Forever churning with countless mills,
Where the lass sings gentle sonnet,
To the chimes of the tardy linnet.

Oh, at home my bed awaits, soft and warm,
My little home, a shade in the storm,
Where the songbird forever sings,
A gentle lullaby of untold kings.

*Oh, at home I wish to sleep,*
*Where I may forever forget to weep,*
*Over the years as a wanderer I did roam,*
*Never more have yearned for home.*

❦

# Sing to me.

*Sing to me as you would to a child,*
*Let your notes caress the very brow of my face,*
*Like the scent of cherry blossoms wild,*
*The bind my heart like scraps of the lace.*

*Sing me the song, songbird.*
*That you sang to my friends over the yonder hills,*
*The song of memories, the song of your words,*
*Sing to me until I have had my fill.*

*Sing me a song that would heal my heart,*
*The little reedy harp stringing from the start,*
*The little lass begs for your gentle refrain,*
*Please sing to me just once again.*

*To your song the years did turn,*
*Yet forever still, for that one thing I yearned ,*
*At work or by the dying embers,*
*Your song was all that I could remember.*

*Sing to me though I am old now,*
*With wrinkles upon on my brow,*
*Sing to me as you would to a child,*
*With the scent of those cherry blossoms wild.*

❧✽❧

# Nightfall

*At nightfall, who is roaming about?*
*A hitchhiker or a drunker I shout,*
*Who dares to stir in this hail?*
*Whose ship by nightfall sets sail?*

*Who whispers, whose voice is heard?*
*Is it nothing or the sound of a bird,*
*Oh, it gnaws on this day is stillness,*
*Sudden screams a bat, in all its shrillness.*

*Oh, nightfall isn't all dull and deary,*
*It's simple, we men are weary,*
*To come out in the first moonlight,*
*For our hands were busy in the harsh daylight.*

*Yet occasionally one or two may stir,*
*Swaddled in coats and warmed up furs,*
*Men with purpose scurry along,*
*Through the dark, deaf and empty throng.*

*Occasionally a lute may play,*
*In the bar where drinkers dance away,*
*And the mockingbird strings a tune,*
*Of perfect notes polished and hewn.*

*Oh, at nightfall another world awakens,*
*Same as ours, they are, the watchmen does harken,*
*His call at nine speaks of noon there,*
*At ten, all the crickets show their wares.*

*So, on and on the little symphony continues,*
*Till the sky glitters with orange hues,*
*At dawn that Little World closes its eyes,*
*While another now stands to rise.*

❦

# The Damsel.

A pretty little damsel as she were,
With profound beauty about her,
She was not a creature cowed or tamed,
She was a feisty little dame.

Many a suitor came from far and wide,
With arrogance upon their every stride,
Who wished to kiss the hand,
Of the fair lady of this land.

Oh, she looked at them with disdain,
Yet her eyes hadn't a trace of vain,
She knew of their endless vice,
Thus, she asked 'em a question wise.

Would you love me the same, if my beauty flies?
If an old woman sits underneath the blue skies,
If that pretty woman that you see now,
Gets wrinkles upon her very brow.

*Would you love me even if my eyes lose their shine?*
*As you would an age-old wine,*
*Would you hold my hand, callused and frail?*
*Would you love me, if my memories fail?*

*Alas, silence breaths upon the entire crowd,*
*It has lost its melodious din loud,*
*No one dares to stare at all,*
*To look into the eyes of the lady, tall.*

*Yet suddenly I spring up, no idea why,*
*And hold her hand and gently cry,*
*My dear, I say, I would love you for eternity,*
*Through age, through life, through infinity.*

# The little flinch.

*With a frightened heart, I said goodbye,*
*To the shadows of the storm's eye,*
*Then I set foot into the winds rumbling, whirling,*
*Alone I walked through all its tumbling.*

*It was not a hawk who could fly alone without worry,*
*It was not the king in its little story,*
*And yet it flew inch by inch,*
*Oh, flew on the little flinch.*

*The wind buffeted it through the air,*
*Each lightning, striking its heart's deepest fears,*
*And yet it still flew without a cry,*
*Choosing just to simply fly.*

*The flinch emerged mightily through the darkened clouds,*
*It flew high in front of the awaiting crowd,*
*A true victory now had been won,*
*For a commoner had now reached the Sun.*

# *The moon shines in her eyes.*

*The moon shines in her eyes,*
*Her iridescent eyes reflect the starry skies,*
*I looked at her from my ragged street,*
*I stare at her face so sweet.*

*Her hair is like the night's embrace,*
*The moonlight falls on her golden face,*
*Lips of pure rose red,*
*Grace the fair lady's head.*

*Her house is by the river's door,*
*Upon the golden sandy shore,*
*Of the towering towers flying high,*
*The manor truly lives in the sky.*

*How can such a lady born of gold,*
*Love a lover, distraught and cold,*
*How can she see the love?*
*That's carried by this poor little dove.*

*Against a lady of great stature, great creed,*
*Alas! This poor heart forgot his breed,*
*Oh, she was a lady so great and fine,*
*Alas! She shall never be mine.*

# The Flower seller.

*Solitary she comes up with her wares,*
*Her brow caressed with all her cares,*
*Yet still with love she sets those flowers,*
*On a ragged cloth in this big bazaar.*

*Her nimble hands gently hold,*
*The needle straight for the marigold,*
*A garland for the God she weaves through the day,*
*A garland for wedding she weaves away.*

*She looks up not at the throng of men,*
*Dawn turns dusk no idea when,*
*Moving not a muscle, a single bone,*
*She seems statue made of stone.*

*A statue on whose feet lay the flowers,*
*Falling from trees in merry showers,*
*In a gown of rags, sits the queen with her flowers,*
*Silently crying, through her lifeless stares.*

# *That's Life.*

*Some are the things we miss,*
*The things that we count,*
*Some of them are wishes,*
*That are always found.*

*Some of them are stories who narrate a tale,*
*While some are ships who set sail are lost to gale,*
*Some fall wayside, some are doves who fly up high,*
*With love upon their wings to the endless skies.*

*Some are short like the breath of air,*
*Some are long like the river's maze,*
*Some are those who give us countlessly glee,*
*While some are those from whom we want to flee.*

*While some are those whom we clutch in darkness,*
*There words gleaming in all their starkness,*
*Whom we let go along with tears,*
*Some are those who reveal our fears.*

# The ballet of song birds and trees

The winds buffet through the air,
The trees take up their dance fair,
The trees look like peacock's feather,
To the song of bird's ballet in this weary weather.

The rustling leaves dance away,
To a gust of wind flying astray,
The tunes reach the crescendo's height,
The songbirds to take up flight.

A valley of birds fills the air,
A twinning dance like a widened snare,
All join in, foe and friend,
A dance of joy till the end.

A ballet forever of songbirds and trees,
A dance similar over the seven seas,
Centuries ago, it was the same,
This symphony is forever untamed.

✿

# Hounds.

*The hounds start to bark,*
*This symphony starts to play in the dark,*
*The cries of mercy of the fawn,*
*Whimpered right before the dawn.*

*The birds take up flight,*
*The vultures circle under the light,*
*Over the stains of red,*
*By the fawn's lifeless head.*

*The wind starts to grieve,*
*The mist still bereaves,*
*The trees avert their eyes,*
*From that kill upon the ice,*

*The hounds lick every bone,*
*The stains upon the stone,*
*They raise their paws dripping red,*
*And howl to the moon shining ahead.*

ꕥ

# Lover.

I look at the old creature,
With misery upon her every feature,
Frail, she knocks every door,
Of every cabin upon the shore.

They say she is a creature born of pain,
That her heart still searches in vain,
Wishing to nurse what's broken apart,
She searches for the one who once held her heart.

I see her at the docks waiting,
Alone, while the sun is setting,
While the winds whisper to her eyes,
She waits on despite with her stippled cries.

The winds to take up this lament tonight,
For the unhappy creature upon their site,
Forever searching across the doors,
She waits for someone who never came ashore.

*I heard the legend in a little rhyme,*
*They say she lost her lover to the time,*
*Yet she waits day and night,*
*Till death would end her plight.*

❦

# The lone traveler.

In the darkened streets,
On the cold broken alley,
Through the mist's blooming heartbeat,
A lone traveler walks silently.

In this dark weary night,
He sits with a cigar for a while,
Underneath the warm lantern light,
In the hearts of simplicity, away from guile.

He has barely a coat to keep warm,
As the walks through the endless storm,
With shoes reduced to shreds,
And pockets full of crumbs of bread.

He does not turn to the drunkard's call,
He chooses to walk straight and tall,
The lone traveler walks hence,
Forever and ever in his reminiscence.

ఌ✾ఌ

# Twilight.

*Prior to the embrace of night,*
*All light is sucked out of the skies,*
*Strings of the song of the Twilight,*
*To the fateful lapwing's cries.*

*The passionate crimson turns to leave,*
*Purple patterns now start to weave,*
*With this odd hue the sky is are filled,*
*Never stopping until the air is stilled.*

*Dawn has turned to dusk through the hands of noon,*
*Dusk turns to night with the shining moon,*
*Twilight stands in the very heart,*
*Keeping these two worlds apart.*

*In reigning glory Twilight stands,*
*Fleeting through upon the land,*
*Through its few hours it changes the weather,*
*Turning this world into another.*

*Uncomplaining it relinquishes power,*
*Behind the night sky is it starts to cower,*
*Engulfed in the darkness of the star in night,*
*Bids goodbye, the gentle Twilight.*

ᔓᔕ✽ᔓᔕ

# Whispering winds.

*The winds whisper to my ears,*
*A song of fury, a song of love,*
*A song dancing through the thousand years,*
*In the orchestra above.*

*They bring faith as the walking glory,*
*To the parched earth who begs in pain,*
*They herald in welcome, the rain clouds fury,*
*The earth begs again for this refrain.*

*The rains walk hand in hand,*
*With gale upon this land,*
*The king of winds too set in motion*
*The farmer's heart in elation.*

*Whispering winds sing this story,*
*Of the rise and fall of their fury,*
*I hear them clearly in my ears,*
*The song of glory through the thousand years.*

ශ✽ශ

# Love

*Love is fickle,*
*Its arms are fake,*
*Through its grin blood does trickle,*
*Into an endless bloody lake.*

*Its promises are lies,*
*Its words, poison,*
*Inside its soulless eyes,*
*Lies hatred's ocean.*

*Its trust are chains,*
*To bind you tight,*
*Its hugs are pains,*
*Holding your flight.*

*Love is an illusion,*
*A dream of the mind,*
*Wish our hearts envision,*
*Forever and never to find.*

ঌ❃ঌ

# Sands of time.

The sands of time, they cry their tears,
Watching the earth turn through years,
Winds of dust sweep these fields,
All things living, all dead, turn to yield.

Trees green and tall, turn to dust,
Their bodies decaying on the ever-shifting crust,
Bodies of men do wither away,
Nothing forever truly stays.

Tall mountains too bow down low,
They are barren tops covered with snow,
Losing the battle to the sword of time,
Life changes with every chime.

The rivers who with might did flow,
Now trickle through the fields where grass did grow,
Nothing resists this pull of time,
My little town to fell too this chime.

*The sands of time fly over the hills,*
*Moving through those abandoned mills,*
*The gates of iron have started to rust,*
*Our playing fields have turned to dust.*

ൿ❦ൿ

# I found her.

*I found her crying,*
*By the silver stream that flowed,*
*The gentle teardrops softly falling,*
*Over the sweetened grass that glowed.*

*Her tears akin to the falling rains,*
*Her cries were like the screams of pain,*
*Like the little fawn in the hunter's snare,*
*She cried of worries and all her cares.*

*Her cries resonated through the darkened woods,*
*Her face covered with the cloth of her hood,*
*Alone with the maple leaves she sings this sonnet,*
*Joins her, the grieving linnet.*

*She cries there alone, untouched by years,*
*She cries her heart swathed in fears,*
*She grieves, she cries of what she lost,*
*She stays on, no matter the cost.*

*I ventured in the woods, one day,*
*By curiosity lead astray,*
*Then I found her, lady of this legend,*
*I found her still crying upon the bend.*

*On and on this road never seems to end,*
*Springing a new path at each bend,*
*Will her cries ever end?*
*Not until she finds someone to mend.*

❦

# I care no more.

*Damn be the consequences,*
*The prophecies spoken hence,*
*I care no more of the trifling part,*
*The broken shrouded worries of heart.*

*No, my heart doesn't bleed anymore,*
*It doesn't nurse a broken sore,*
*It has left the crack, the crevice of pain,*
*It has let go of the sea of worries that pertain.*

*No more do I cower from the sword of fate,*
*I am done hiding forever to wait,*
*What comes next, I care no more,*
*For with these broken wings I must learn to soar.*

*Adversity, misfortunes do not last,*
*I won't brood about my past,*
*What's done can't be undone,*
*It's new me, it's my turn.*

# Siren.

Oh, sailor head my song,
I call to you from the ocean's depth,
I know your yearning, your desires strong,
Give in to the sea's stormy breath.

Fear not of its stormy waves,
Look not at the endless graves,
Think of your vow, away from prow,
Let not worries crowd your brow.

Don't fear as the water choke your throat,
You need not look earning at your little boat,
Do not try to fight its flow,
Close your eyes and simply let go.

Do not fear the darkened troves,
Nor the poison coral coves,
Do not fear death's embrace,
Let light gently vanish off your face.

ᔓᔕ✻ᔓᔕ

# Surrender.

*Close your eyes,*
*Though I know it's hard,*
*Let the wind crumble,*
*Your house of cards.*

*Sheath your sword, lower it down,*
*Though you may call it cowardice,*
*Leave this fight, leave the crown,*
*Do not pay such a price.*

*Surrender now,*
*For its futile to fight,*
*Drop the crown of your brow,*
*Let the darkness engulf crown's glorious light.*

*Fear not for your armies are slain,*
*And you stand alone,*
*My sword doesn't shy from pain,*
*It can softly cut your bones.*

*Hence as a fallen king,*
*Leave my city shores,*
*The arms of exile softly sing,*
*To the fallen king of this lore.*

ఌ✽ఌ

# Maybe.

May the sunset kiss you good night,
May the darkness hide you in her arm,
May you never ponder why,
You were never loved by them.

May the stars you fondly seek,
Come to find you in your dreams,
May each day of your week,
Be glittered with golden sun beams.

May your heart never know the sorrow,
That sings with the passing of tomorrow,
May clouds of worry never shroud your face,
Of tears you should know no trace.

May you live with jewels and glory,
The queen of your little story,
May you never think and remember,
My name, lost to the dying embers.

ಣ✽ಣ

# *Six broken hearts.*

*Six broken strings,*
*Of the lute that we used to play,*
*Twelve broken wings,*
*Of the birds who flied astray.*

*Six empty cups, erectly stay,*
*Upon the empty table left standing,*
*A ghost of a long-gone day,*
*A day of broken understandings.*

*Six broken bonds of the heart,*
*Six brothers whole apart,*
*The wind split their different roads,*
*Each brother stranded at separate crossroads.*

*The six heart strings shriveled away,*
*The broken lute ceased to play,*
*For that day, brother turned on brother,*
*Hatred in eyes burnt for each other.*

*Six broken brothers then died alone,*
*Scattered stood their solitary gravestone,*
*Six broken hearts, never met to say,*
*Forgive me brother for that fateless day.*

ꕥ

# Pain.

*Do you know what is pain?*
*Have you ever listened to this refrain?*
*A stab or cut truly counts nothing,*
*It's the ache that shatters your wings.*

*At night when you beg yourself to hold together,*
*When your soul screams in misery,*
*When you can't grieve, but must rather,*
*Weave on with this story.*

*When you drown but cannot die,*
*When you wish to scream yet cannot cry,*
*That is pain that truly breaks,*
*And leaves you broken by death's lake.*

*When you are hurt but no one comes,*
*To sing the ache away, a little hum,*
*When you are alone with a broken heart,*
*That's the pain that breaks you apart.*

ᔓᔕ❦ᔓᔕ

# Burning desire.

*Your face is gentle, true and pure,*
*You are the object of my desire,*
*It is your allure,*
*That ignites this burning fire.*

*It is not your face that pulls me to you,*
*Rather it is your actions, kind and true,*
*I love you with whole of my heart,*
*Your grace, your beauty, truly is an art.*

*My heart begs for your gentle voice,*
*Your soft laugh and splendid poise,*
*I love you; I love you dear,*
*But you do not feel the same, I fear.*

∽✽∽

# Frightful chains.

Two chains they hold my heart,
Chaining it down from the start,
A frantic heart beats wildly against the bones,
A broken feeling whilst all alone.

My head is swimming in a forelone haze,
My eyes can't break of this frightful daze,
A lingering fear splits my mind,
To my own self my eyes turn blind.

It is with this cage I must reconcile,
In its arms going quite senile,
The cage of longing expectations,
I reside with loss of jubilation.

# Teenage.

A new Dawn, a subtle change,
This journey of teenage,
From a little girl to a blossoming lady,
Ever-changing moods and body.

Where friends are not so close,
Were parents being near yet far,
The fear, the expectations,
And the pressure to perform.

The despair, the independence,
The dependence and ignorance,
The fitting in or maybe not,
The anger, the jest, the fights, the crush and heart breaks.

My journey through the thoughts,
Some pleasant, some crescent,
How do I know what's right, what's wrong,
For in my thoughts, I travel alone.

# Twilight's heart

She belonged not to the roaring day,
Nor did the night claim her as her own,
Her hues, a war of violet and grey,
Bare stood her daintily throne.

The poor little thing devoid of ego,
No bejeweled stars nor misty glow,
That was Twilight with a heart pure and sublime,
Painted in shades of colorful hue, without a rhyme.

That was Twilight who loved without condition
Who hid away her heart-breaking renditions,
Her beauty unsung, her grace unpraised,
Yet her selfless love, forever blazed.

She loved the wonderful glorious Earth,
And the men never praised her worth,
Between the world's, her throne stood bare,
She was Twilight, gentle and rare.

∽❦∽

# Solitary shadows

I walk alone thru an empty forest,
With no soul to walk abreast,
The trees look down in a mocking way,
They are together and together they sway.

I travel alone, only my shadow for company,
As if a timeless, wordless, empty symphony,
Oh! I do wish I could be found by others,
People I could call friends or lovers.

Till then with my shadow, I will walk alone,
On a solitary cold path of stone,
One day I hope for a friend to meet,
Till then I will walk on with my own feet.

Oh, my shadow, please do forgive,
For sure, I know you will never leave,
What will I do with the so-called friends?
Who would leave me broken at every bend?

ഗ✽ഗ

# Dying

At the last breath,
By the silver wreath,
Reminiscence,
Of a long-gone joyous essence.

A vagabond merchant as I,
Built my riches and towers high,
Yet I too could not run away,
From 'age' that walks behind anyway.

Yet as I lay on the death's door,
I find myself upon a lonely moor,
With no one to grieve and weep,
As I fell into this eternal sleep.

Finally, death reached me,
To him, an answer I beseeched with a plea,
He asked me if I did repent,
Told me to look at my life so spent.

*Lies, deceit and waylay,*
*My life dwelled in the darkness's untold sway,*
*No empathy, no love, no respect,*
*That's how my life was spent.*

*Death answered me, showed the mirror*
*The course of my life he showed, all my errors,*
*The reason why no love was given,*
*Why I was forgotten & never forgiven.*

❧✾❧

# Not Love But...

Once I was reading through the pages of a scattered history,
When I chanced upon a broken story,
And I found the same story repeated page after page,
A hidden tale pertains, age after age, like a mirage.

It started with the king whose heart was broken,
No woman nor love, caused it to weaken,
Shattered dreams of his, to regain lost glory,
Led him to the tragic end of his life's story.

The tale moved to a general proud,
He dreamt to stand apart from the crowd,
Crushed hopes of his, killed him unmerciful,
It was not love but his dreams were unfaithful.

Then the story moved to a dancer great,
Who had much glory written to her fate,
She dreamt to perform in the court of kings,
But broken dreams snatched her soul on its wings.

*Then I knew not love but broken dreams bleed the heart,*
*Broken, snatched dreams break it into pieces apart,*
*Not love but crushing of the dreams whatever they may be,*
*Are the ways to drown a heart in misery's sea.*

# The Tempest

*In the merry skies of weeping blue,*
*The lightning crackles a fatal dance,*
*From the erring blackened hue,*
*The rain falls in a blissful trance.*

*The furious night bond through the storms,*
*Cast the nightly shade,*
*A war of blood, a war of life forms,*
*In the scary starry glade.*

*The thunder roars with the mighty voice,*
*Their fury forever grows,*
*The slashing rains ferociously trails,*
*Drowning the forever woes.*

*Now and then, the sky is torn,*
*By a shard of lightning, in this murderous night,*
*That's how the storm is born,*
*A kingly storm, a tempest with all its might.*

*Alone in the corner, trembling, soaking wet,*
*Lies the little girl waiting her fate.*
*Pleading with the tempest,*
*"Enough", please put me to eternal rest.*

❦

# Her letters

*Her letters I read them still,*
*Sitting right by the broken window sill,*
*Again and again, I find the warmth,*
*I do not stop till I have my fill.*

*Her letters are not addressed to me,*
*They are to someone across the sea,*
*It seems she never sent them to the mail ferry,*
*Never had the courage to send them on their journey.*

*I wonder why, when so beautifully written,*
*With love and kindness gently smitten,*
*Why they were never sent?*
*Why in the dark attic their life was spent?*

*In her words, I see her soul,*
*Young and free like an innocent foal,*
*I can picture her hand gliding across the page,*
*Lost in her thoughts, thinking of his image.*

*I read her gentle flickering words,*
*Each as fleeting as a flying bird,*
*I say to myself, feeling the emotions,*
*I would have loved a mind like hers with passion.*

ᔓ❃ᔓ

# Some days

*Somedays, we'll laugh,*
*Somedays, we'll cry,*
*Somedays we are broken in half,*
*Somedays we simply question, why?*

*Somedays we'll laugh at our own sorrows,*
*Somedays we'll weep at passing of tomorrow,*
*Somedays we'll dance gladly in the rain,*
*Somedays we'll do so to hide our pain.*

*Somedays we will beg sleep to come,*
*Somedays we'll dance to the shanty's hum,*
*Somedays we'll laugh at bygone pasts,*
*Somedays we'll hold on to moments, too little to last.*

*Somedays we'll get reverently drunk and high,*
*Somedays tears will fall through our eyes,*
*Somedays we'll be at the brink, holding a knife,*
*Somedays we'll be oblivious to the ways of life.*

*Somedays we'll dance through the sun kissed clay,*
*Somedays we'll be on a solitary path, lead astray,*
*Somedays we'll cry at the simplest of things,*
*Somedays we'll fly high with our broken wings.*

*Somedays we'll heal, some days we will break,*
*Somedays in dreams we will frightfully wake,*
*Somedays we'll laugh and somedays we'll weep,*
*In the end, someday we'll all return to eternal sleep.*

*The Life continues........... The way it is........... That's Life.*

*Hope.....That's Life.....*

www.ingramcontent.com/pod-product-compliance
Lightning Source LLC
LaVergne TN
LVHW091047150826
845673LV00002B/489

* 9 7 9 8 8 9 6 1 0 6 5 4 8 *